Hands-On History Projects

Integrating History and Language Arts

Author:	Joyce Stulgis Blalock
Illustrator:	Ron Blalock
Editor:	Mary Dieterich
Proofreaders:	Alexis Fey and Margaret Brown

COPYRIGHT © 2020 Mark Twain Media, Inc.

ISBN 978-1-62223-817-0

Printing No. CD-405049

Mark Twain Media, Inc., Publishers
Distributed by Carson-Dellosa Publishing LLC

Table of Contents

Introduction to the Teacher

Hands-On History Projects is a ready-to-use collection of social studies lessons that combine historical and geographical knowledge with writing. It is the perfect way to build important concepts in social studies while developing students' abilities to express themselves orally and in writing.

The Projects

This book presents lessons that feature time periods from ancient civilizations to the future, with a strong emphasis on American history. Many lessons can be used or adapted to several different historical periods. The projects also present a variety of options. Some of the projects are written products (letters, stories, journal), some are graphic presentations (diagrams, murals, maps, charts), and some are oral presentations. With this variety, students will never be bored, and teachers will be able to assess student understanding of the topics with many different project-based products.

Teacher's Instructions

This section provides brief overviews of the lessons. A description of the project, a listing of materials, and information about presenting the lesson are provided for each project. Materials needed are for each student or group, unless otherwise noted. This gives you everything you need to present the lesson in one convenient location.

Lesson Guides

Each lesson guide gives students a clear outline of what they are to do. The Assignment Guidelines present a brief overview and step-by-step instructions that take students from just thinking about the topic to completing the project. Each lesson also includes a historical background section, sample writings, or a sample of the chart or diagram, thus giving students additional direction.

Research

All lessons require students to complete some kind of research. Sometimes it is specified how or how much they should do, but often the instruction only says to find out about their topic. While students may get a lot of information from their social studies texts, you will want to have several other sources of information available for them in the classroom or give them time online and in the library to find the needed information.

Group or Individual?

Some of the lessons are clearly written for group production, while others are best done on an individual basis. Some lessons may be done either by a small group or by individuals working by themselves.

Outstanding Projects

Students should follow this classroom-proven technique for producing successful projects. (1) Select a topic. (2) Do the research. (3) Follow the directions and the lesson guide. (4) Complete an outstanding project. It's easy, and it's effective. You will be impressed with the outstanding projects students will produce as well as the original thinking they will use to produce these projects. This approach not only keeps students excited about social studies, it builds writing skills, speaking skills, thinking skills, and cooperation. It will become a welcome supplement to your social studies curriculum.

Project Instructions for the Teacher

Ancient Civilizations (p. 10)

Project Output – A poster comparing four ancient civilizations

Materials – large poster board, colored markers or pencils, glue, atlas

Process – For this lesson, students need to have access to research materials on ancient civilizations. You may have students work with a partner to do this assignment, but they can also work alone. If they work alone, it may take longer than one week to complete.

Ancient Egypt (p. 11)

Project Output – A poster showing various aspects of Egyptian life

Materials – poster board, glue, colored markers

Process – This week students will be studying various aspects of Egyptian life. You may choose to visit the library for two days, or you can make references on Egyptian life available in the classroom. You may want to assign four aspects to each group to prevent duplication. The students will be working in pairs or in groups of three. Sharing time is necessary for this project. As an extended activity, you may want students to construct a model showing the information they are presenting.

King Tut's Tomb (p. 12)

Project Output – Settings and stories that take place in King Tut's tomb

Materials – writing paper

Process – Students will work alone on this project. Using King Tut's tomb as the setting for the beginning or ending of a story, they will write three different paragraphs describing the surroundings of the tomb. They will then choose the best one and develop it into a story.

Athens & Sparta (p. 13)

Project Output – Two story boards illustrating lives of a Spartan child and an Athenian child

Materials – one poster board (cut in half lengthwise), markers, ruler, research materials

Process – This week students will be working in pairs to produce two storyboards: one that portrays the life of a Spartan youngster and another that shows the life of an Athenian youngster. They should draw several pictures and add written text that explains the pictures.

Writing Myths (p. 14)

Project Output – An original myth

Materials – writing paper, poster board, colored pencils or pens

Process – This lesson works well if it is presented after the students have studied myths. They must have some knowledge of how myths are written and the basis for them and should have read a few myths before they begin. After they are aware of the style in which myths are written, they may begin planning to write their own myths. When they complete their stories, they should illustrate them, mount them on poster board, and share them with the class.

Ancient Greece & Rome (p. 15)

Project Output – A poster comparing various aspects of the Greek and Roman civilizations

Materials – poster board, marking pens

Process – This week the students will be researching the Greek and Roman Empires. They will work with a partner or in cooperative learning groups and will find information about certain characteristics of each civilization. Then they will transfer this information to a poster. The poster can be either large or small but should be illustrated in full color. The students can share their posters when completed.

A Manor Newspaper (p. 16)

Project Output – A newspaper page reflecting life on a manor during the Middle Ages.

Materials – poster board, white paper, glue, scissors

Process – For this lesson, students will work in groups. Each group will be responsible for writing one page of a newspaper. Each person in the group should write at least one article. Students should copy their articles onto heavy paper and glue these to larger paper to make the newspaper format.

A Knight's Story (p. 17)

Project Output – An original story that shows the steps one went through to become a knight
Materials – drawing paper, colored pens or pencils, writing paper
Process – For this week's projects students will need several books with information about knighthood. In addition to writing a story that tells the events that lead to a young man obtaining knighthood, students will make an illustration of their knight and will make a coat of arms.

A Knight in Shining Armor (p. 18)

Project Output – A time line and a complete story of a knight
Materials – strips of paper
Process – Before starting this project, students should do some reading about manors and the feudal system. They will be making a story plan by making a time line. The story will tell about the courageous deeds of a knight.

Renaissance Biographies (p. 19)

Project Output – A written biography and oral presentation that highlights the achievements of an important person in the Renaissance
Materials – index cards, writing paper, drawing paper, colored pencils or pens
Process – For this lesson, students may work by themselves or in groups. They will research an important person from the Renaissance and record the information on index cards. They will use this information to write a biography of the person and will make an oral presentation.

Renaissance Diaries (p. 20)

Project Output – Diary entries of an important Renaissance person
Materials – writing paper
Process – For this lesson, students need to be familiar with the life of one person from the Renaissance. Several people are listed in the lesson guide, but you may want to offer other choices. They will be writing four diary entries that reflect on events in the life of the person they have chosen.

Art of the Renaissance (p. 21)

Project Output – A resumé for a Renaissance artist
Materials – drawing paper, paint, writing paper
Process – Students will be studying the artists of the Renaissance. They will be writing a resumé and making pictures in the artist's style that they will present in a mock interview for a position with the Medici family. You can assign an artist to each student if you want to avoid duplication. Some of the well-known artists include Leonardo da Vinci, Michelangelo Buonarotti, Sandro Botticelli, Filippo Lippi, Perugino, Andrea Mantegna, Vittore Carpaccio, Raphael, Titian, Lica Signorelli, Giorgione, Lorenzo Lotto, Tintoretto, and Benvenuto Cellini.

Columbus Calls for Adventurers (p. 22)

Project Output – A brochure calling for adventurers to join Columbus' second voyage
Materials – 9" x 18" drawing paper, colored markers, black pen
Process – For this lesson, you may want to have students working with partners. They will do research on Columbus and make a brochure asking for volunteers for Columbus' second voyage to the New World. The printing on the brochure should be done in black pen, highlighted with color illustrations.

Great Explorers (p. 23)

Project Output – A monologue asking for funding for an upcoming expedition
Materials – writing paper
Process – For this lesson, students will write a speech given by one of the great explorers. In this speech, the explorer must tell of his travels in a passionate manner because this lecture will hopefully bring him monetary support for future explorations. Students will present their speeches to the class, dressed in costumes if they wish.

Native North Americans (p. 24)

Project Output – A chart comparing three different Native American groups

Materials – poster board, paper, glue, colored markers

Process – Students may work in pairs for this project. You will need information on several different Native American tribes, showing how they lived hundreds of years ago. Students will create a poster that will compare three different tribes from different geographical locations. Some additional tribes to consider would be the Yakima, Kickapoo, Miami, Shawnee, Choctaw, Nez Perce, Ute, Comanche, Pawnee, and Crow.

The First Thanksgiving (p. 25)

Project Output – An original story set in Plymouth during the first Thanksgiving

Materials – writing paper

Process – In addition to the information that is provided for students on the lesson guide, you may want to have other resources available. Students will write a story from the perspective of someone who would have been present at the first Thanksgiving.

A Colonial Newspaper (p. 26)

Project Output – A newspaper telling about life in the early colonies

Materials – large paper, writing paper, glue, colored pencils or pens

Process – For this assignment, students will work in pairs. They will create a newspaper page that will show what life was like in the early colonies. For one article, they will interview a classmate who will pretend to be a recent immigrant and will tell what life is like for him or her. Other articles should reflect events that did or could have happened in the colony.

Colonial Life Play (p. 27)

Project Output – A play that takes place in a colonial home and shows events that could have happened at this time

Materials – writing paper, large sheet of paper for backdrop, paint or chalk

Process – Students will work in groups to write and produce plays about colonial life. All plays will be performed before the same large backdrop of a room in a colonial home. It works well to clear a large area (about 12 square feet) of the room and lay out a large sheet or a piece of paper. Throughout the week, have one person from each group come to the area each day to work on the backdrop.

Come to the Colonies (p. 28)

Project Output – A poster advertising life in the colonies

Materials – poster paper, colored pencils and pens, crayons

Process – Students may work by themselves or with a partner for this project. They are to research an early American colony and make a poster. The poster should tell about the colony and entice settlers to move to the colony.

The Revolution Begins (p. 29)

Project Output – written explanations, a short report, and an original story, all detailing the events that led to the Revolutionary War

Materials – writing paper, large index cards, information about the Revolutionary War and the people and groups involved in the war

Process – This project has four different parts. Students will be studying the events that led to the American Revolutionary War. They will explain and analyze several different events, make a time line, write a short report, and create an original story. You may need more than the four days that are detailed in the lesson guide for students to complete, revise, and edit their final stories.

Reporting on the Revolution (p. 30)

Project Output – A news show highlighting the events of a Revolutionary War battle

Materials – writing paper, optional items: props, large butcher paper, paint or markers, video equipment

Process – For this lesson, students need access to information on the Revolutionary War battles. You can have students work in groups, assigning each group to a different battle. Each group will write a script that incorporates facts, events, and fictional commentary on the war. They will make their presentation as a news show. The day of the presentation, you can videotape each presentation. You can also have students create a backdrop for this show using a large piece of paper.

Life After the Revolutionary War (p. 31)

Project Output – Letters to a fictional friend describing life after the Revolutionary War

Materials – writing paper

Process – For this week's project, students will have to research the events following the Revolutionary War. Some facts are listed on the lesson guide. They will write several letters to a fictional friend who lives in Europe, telling about the events of the time. While the letters should include information students have found in their research, they can add some fictional events or personal commentaries.

Studying the Constitution (p. 32)

Project Output – An oral defense of one branch of the government

Materials – writing paper, reference books or online references

Process – This week students will divide into three groups. Each group will be assigned a different branch of the government to defend. The premise is that there will be a referendum to change the Constitution and they are to convince voters to keep this branch of the government. This project might take more than a week to complete.

The Bill of Rights (p. 33)

Project Output – Various projects that allow students to analyze the Bill of Rights

Materials – chart paper, marking pens, writing paper

Process – This week's lesson is divided into four parts. Students will work in groups. On the first day, the groups will analyze what would happen if there were no laws, courts, or law enforcers. On the second day, the groups will write their own bill of rights. On the third day, each group will study a type of government in

another country. The final day, they will discuss the responsibilities of citizens. You will need to have lots of chart paper available so each group can record their ideas. You will also need to schedule sharing time at the end of each day.

The Haunting of Monticello (p. 34)

Project Output – An original ghost story set in Monticello

Materials – writing paper, reference materials

Process – It only takes a bit of imagination and a love of ghost stories for this lesson to be a success. Thomas Jefferson's life and his love for his wife and for Monticello make fertile ground for a haunting story. Before beginning the writing, students should have information about Jefferson and Monticello. It is also good to discuss the characteristics of an effective ghost story or read a couple of these stories.

American Industry & Transportation (p. 35)

Project Output – A written report and project on an innovation of the 1800s

Materials – writing paper, index cards, paint, poster paper, small boxes, markers, construction paper

Process – This lesson may take two weeks. It involves researching an invention of the 1800s. The first week, students should research their topics and write a report. The second week, they should select a project and complete it. Students may work with partners. You may add other topics, or students may select other topics that interest them.

The Abolition Movement (p. 36)

Project Output – An oral presentation about various topics related to abolition and the Civil War

Materials – writing paper, reference materials

Process – Students will need access to several print or online reference books about the Civil War for this project. You may want to assign topics so there is no duplication. After doing their research, students will make an oral presentation about the topic or person they have researched.

The Civil War Explodes (p. 37)

Project Output – A time line, character cutout, game board, and quilt square depicting events and people from the Civil War

Materials – drawing paper, colored pencils and pens, cardboard, strips of paper

Process – This project will take two weeks and students will work with partners. They will be doing several projects: a cutout of a Civil War character that will be mounted on a bulletin board, a time line, a square for a class quilt, and a game. You may assign famous people and battles so there is no duplication. You may also choose to add other famous people and events.

Civil War Journals (p. 38)

Project Output – A journal chronicling a soldier's experiences during the Civil War

Materials – writing paper, paper or materials for journal cover

Process – For this project, students will need a good background in Civil War history. They will also need access to references about the Civil War battles and important leaders. The final project will be a journal telling about the author's war experiences. Since this journal is probably something that the soldier would have carried around with him through several battles, students will want to make their paper and cover look old and worn.

Civil War Battles (p. 39)

Project Output – A mural of a Civil War battle

Materials – large paper (at least 2' by 3'), index cards, drawing and coloring materials

Process – For this lesson, students will research a Civil War battle and make a mural that includes a picture of the battle and information about the battle. They will need to research the particular battle. This assignment works best if students work in groups. This project could be used for battles in any war.

Speech Writing for President Lincoln (p. 40)

Project Output – A speech that Lincoln could have given before signing the Emancipation Proclamation

Materials – writing paper, reference materials, props (optional)

Process – It is necessary that students know the contents of the Emancipation Proclamation to do this assignment. They will be working alone to write a speech. For the presentation, however, they may choose to enlist others to help them make their presentation realistic. If students' presentations are videotaped they seem to do a better job of writing and presenting.

Reconstruction (p. 41)

Project Output – A talk show highlighting several different perspectives of life during the Reconstruction

Materials – writing paper, reference materials, costumes (optional), video equipment (optional)

Process – Students will work in cooperative groups for this lesson. They will develop a script for a talk show that they will deliver before an imaginary audience at the College of William and Mary in Williamsburg. To do this, they will need to research the Reconstruction Era. On the day students present their talk shows, costumes must be worn. You may want to videotape the talk show presentation.

The Gold Rush (p. 42)

Project Output – Poster telling about gold mining during the mid-1800s

Materials – poster board, colored markers

Process – For this lesson, students need information about the search for gold during the mid-1800s in America. They will make a chart presenting information about the Gold Rush.

The Westward Movement (p. 43)

Project Output – A letter defending a decision to move West or stay in the East

Materials – writing paper

Process – For this lesson, students are given the situation that they live in the East during the 1840s and have to decide if they will stay where they are and deal with the economic hardships that people faced at that time or move to Oregon. Each decision presents some positive and negative features. After students have listed all the problems associated with each decision, they should decide what they would do and then write a letter that explains their decision. It would be helpful to have a class discussion about the reasons why someone might decide to move or decide to stay before students begin their writing.

Men of the West (p. 44)

Project Output – A newspaper article about one of the famous men of the western frontier
Materials – drawing and writing paper
Process – Students will select one man who lived and worked in the West during the 1800s and will write a newspaper article that might have appeared in a newspaper at this time.

The Dispossessed People (p. 45)

Project Output – A letter from a Native American's point of view
Materials – writing paper
Process – For this lesson, students will research how the western expansion affected native tribes living in the West. They will then write a letter to the leaders of the government expressing their concerns and asking for certain rights for their people. The letter can be accompanied by a map showing where the tribe lived.

Come to America, Land of Opportunity (p. 46)

Project Output – A poster encouraging people to come to America
Materials – large poster board, colored pens and pencils, research materials
Process – For this lesson, students will be doing research on America at the turn of the twentieth century. They will make a poster advertising the opportunities in the United States. For this they will need a variety of print or online research materials. They will work with a partner. In addition to the text on the poster, they will need to add original illustrations.

Silent Movie Making (p. 47)

Project Output – A script for a silent movie depicting an historical event
Materials – writing paper, large pieces of paper for dialogue, video equipment, clips from silent movies (optional)

Process – If you can find an old silent movie to show before this lesson, it would help students understand the limitations of early movie production. It will also be necessary to arrange for the use of video equipment for several days. To show the dialogue, students will need to write the words on large pieces of stiff paper that will be held in front of the camera in lieu of speaking. If they add music, piano music is best. You may want to suggest other historic events to portray.

Revolutionary Transportation (p. 48)

Project Output – A drawn and written comparison of two different models of automobiles and two different airplanes
Materials – index cards, drawing paper, writing paper
Process – This lesson is most effective if students work with a partner. It works well if you are studying machines in science or the growth of technology in social studies. Students need to be able to find detailed information about the automobiles and airplanes they choose. After researching, students will draw their automobiles and airplanes and prepare a written comparison of the two models.

African-American Heroes (p. 49)

Project Output – A portfolio showing the accomplishments of a famous African American
Materials – construction paper, writing paper, drawing paper, pencils and markers
Process – For this lesson, students will have to consult print or online biographies of African Americans. They will be creating materials that represent a person's accomplishments, feelings, and most important life events and putting these materials in a portfolio. They will then make an oral presentation of the materials. This lesson could also be used to highlight the accomplishments of other minorities. In addition to the people listed on the assignment sheet, some other prominent African Americans include Joe Lewis, P. B. S. Pinchback, A. Philip Randolph, Paul Robeson, Booker T. Washington, Jackie Robinson, and George Washington Carver.

Famous Women (p. 50)

Project Output – A comparison between a famous American woman and an important woman in the student's life

Materials – writing material, large paper

Process – For this lesson, students will choose an important American woman and research her life. They will then select a woman from their own life whom they admire. They will write several questions that are inspired by their research and use the questions to interview the woman in their life. Finally, they will compare the two women, being sensitive not to diminish the accomplishments of the person they know even though she has not achieved notoriety, but to show similarities between their goals, interests, upbringing, or education. In addition to the women listed on the lesson guide, students could research Mildred Didrikson "Babe" Zaharias, Wilma Rudolph, Elizabeth Blackwell, Maria Mitchell, Sylvia Earle, Shirley Chisholm, Marian Anderson, Louise Boyd, Margaret Higgins Sanger, Francis Perkins, Julia Morgan, Alice Hamilton, Sarah Breedlove Walker, Jane Addams, Emma Lazarus, Louisa May Alcott, Mary Harris Jones, Susan B. Anthony, Helen Keller, Grandma Moses, Pocahontas, Catherine Littlefield Greene, Sacajawea, Lucretia Coffin Mott, Dorothea Dix, Harriet Beecher Stowe, or Mary Baker Eddy.

Comparing Presidents (p. 51)

Project Output – Speech chronicling a president's life

Materials – writing paper, research material, video equipment (optional)

Process – Students will work with a partner for this project. Each person will select a president and write a speech as if they are the president's biographer. They will then give the speeches and make a comparison of the presidents. This is a good lesson to videotape.

Propaganda (p. 52)

Project Output – A poster showing examples of different propaganda techniques

Materials – magazines, newspapers, poster board, glue, marking pens

Process – This lesson could be used when studying almost any war, particularly World War II, or when studying advertising. Before students begin this project, you should discuss propaganda, giving examples of different techniques and explaining how they are used in various areas of everyday life. Students may work alone or with a partner.

Fact & Opinion (p. 53)

Project Output – Questions and an essay to distinguish between fact and opinion

Materials – writing paper, newspapers or news magazines, access to news sites online

Process – For this lesson, students will need to consult newspapers, news magazines, and online news sites to develop an awareness of current events. They will write 20 questions, some of which will be factual questions and some of which will be questions to elicit opinions related to the factual questions. They will then interview a classmate, asking him or her the questions. Based on the answers to the questions, students will write an essay. It works best if you assign the partners for this project.

Points of View (p. 54)

Project Output – A dialogue expressing two opposing points of view on the same issue

Materials – writing paper, research materials

Process – For this project, students may select any historical event that would have generated two different points of view. They will write a dialogue that expresses these viewpoints and will make an oral presentation of the dialogue.

Migration (p. 55)

Project Output – A map and written explanation of a people's migration

Materials – drawing paper, poster paper, colored pens and pencils, writing paper, atlas

Process – Students can choose any human migration for this project. They will make a map that shows where the people migrated from and where they went. They will also write an explanation of why the people migrated and what the consequences of the move were.

Earth Geography (p. 56)

Project Output – Five different projects to develop an awareness of the geography of the earth

Materials – maps of the world, your city, and the United States, writing paper, drawing paper

Process – This project is divided into five parts, each one focusing on the geography of the world and different regions. Students will need to refer to various maps to complete each project. For three of the projects, they will be creating a written description. They will choose one of these pieces and revise and edit it on the last day. The other projects are maps.

Regions of Our Country (p. 57)

Project Output – Symbols for a U.S. map and diagram of regional characteristics

Materials – drawing paper, colored pencils and pens, large poster paper, atlas

Process – This project will take some time to prepare. You will need to make a large outline map of the United States where students will make symbols and attach them. Students will work in groups, each group being responsible for a different feature on the map. Each group will need an atlas. In addition to the large class map, each group will prepare a diagram that compares whichever feature they have been assigned in the five regions.

Time Traveler (p. 58)

Project Output – An original story

Materials – writing paper

Process – This lesson can be adapted to any time period in history. Students begin in one period of history they have studied and then travel via a time machine to another time period. This lesson works best if students have studied both the time periods they choose to write about. After the students have written their accounts of time traveling, it's fun if they share their stories.

A Snowy Adventure (p. 59)

Project Output – An original story set in the snow in any time of history

Materials – writing paper

Process – This is a good lesson to use during winter. It can be used with any time in history, though it works best if students choose a time in history they are familiar with. The objective of the story should be not only to reflect life at some point in history but also to use sensory references that will allow readers to experience the snowy adventure by appealing to several of their senses.

A Yard Sale Treasure (p. 60)

Project Output – An original story

Materials – writing paper

Process – This lesson is good to tie in with current events or a unit on contemporary problems. Students should have a good sense of events in the world and problems that exist in their neighborhoods, city, country, and world. They will be writing a list of things that they would like to change about the world and then writing a story that explains five of these problems and precisely how they would solve those problems.

Designing the Future (p. 61)

Project Output – A design for the city of the future

Materials – large, heavy drawing paper, colored pens and pencils, writing paper

Process – For this lesson, students need to have some knowledge of the structure and function of a city. They need to be able to identify some of the problems that currently face their city and be able to use creative thinking to pose solutions for the future. They will work in groups to design their new cities and make maps, diagrams, and illustrations to graphically show what the cities will be like.

Name: _____ Date: _____

Ancient Civilizations

Assignment Guidelines

For this week's project you are to do the following assignments.

1. Use as many resources as possible to find information about the following ancient civilizations: **Canaan**, **Babylon**, **Sumeria**, and **Assyria**.
2. Find out where these people lived, how they dressed, what kinds of houses they had, what weapons they used, and what their religious beliefs were.
3. Draw a map of the area where this civilization existed. You may find that their regions overlapped in some cases.
4. Place all this information on a large poster, with a section for each civilization. If possible, add an illustration of each characteristic you found, along with the written information. For instance, a picture of the houses used by this group would accompany information on houses.
5. Then write the common characteristics shared by all of the groups in the area at the bottom of the poster.
6. Be prepared to share your chart with the class and discuss the basic characteristics of each group.

Comparison of Ancient Civilizations

Canaan	Babylon	Sumeria	Assyria
Map	Map	Map	Map
Characteristics of this civilization	Characteristics of this civilization	Characteristics of this civilization	Characteristics of this civilization

Common Characteristics

Name: _____   Date: _____

Ancient Egypt

Assignment Guidelines

This week you will be researching life in ancient Egypt. The following is a list of your assignments for the week:

1. Research the ancient Egyptians, finding out all that you can about their daily life. You should find out about their clothing, houses, temples, pyramids, weapons, tools, musical instruments, art, or any other topic you find interesting.
2. Either your teacher will assign four different aspects of Egyptian life or you will choose four of these aspects to research in more depth.
3. Write paragraphs containing the most pertinent information about each of the areas you have been assigned.
4. Transfer this information onto a piece of poster board.
5. Choose an appropriate way of illustrating each topic in full color, using markers or crayons. You may want to use a layout similar to the one below, or you may have a better way of showing the four areas of Egyptian life.
6. Finally, share the poster and information with the class. You may use drama to share your information if you wish, but all members of your group have to take part in the presentation.

Aspects of Egyptian Life

Temples of Egypt	Houses of Egypt
Illustration	Illustration
Descriptive paragraph	Descriptive paragraph
Art of Egypt	**Mummification**
Illustration	Illustration
Descriptive paragraph	Descriptive paragraph

Name: _____ Date: _____

King Tut's Tomb

Assignment Guidelines

This week you will be writing three detailed descriptive settings using King Tut's tomb as the place where you begin or end a story.

1. Research King Tutankhamen and his tomb.
2. Use his tomb as the setting for three different stories. Write three different paragraphs that are either the beginnings or endings of stories, describing the surroundings in detail. The three sample settings below will help you think of ideas. To get the different settings, you can vary the season of the year, the time of day, or the mood.
3. After you have written the beginning or ending of three stories, choose the one you like the best and write the complete story.

Sample Setting 1

Carter had waited years for this moment. Even the sand on the steps under his shoes became apparent to him, so keen were his senses. His guide assistant, Mogadia, placed the crowbar in the door jam and pulled back with all his might. A great cracking noise followed, and finally it opened. There before them lay the dust-filled darkness that Carter knew was Tut's final resting place. They stepped forward and suddenly detected a strange chemical-like odor.

Sample Setting 2

He awoke at the deafening sound and found himself in darkness. He couldn't remember falling asleep. He knew he had to get up but he felt so weak. He managed to pull himself up and felt around for a lantern or torch. Suddenly, a bright shaft of white light poured through the room and the silhouette of a tall man appeared in the open doorway. The man in the doorway took one step forward, waving his arms to push the cobwebs from in front of his path.

Sample Setting 3

She left the hotel, dressed for the cold desert air, late that night in the mysterious city of Cairo. Because it was winter, each breath was a vapor trail. She ran across the soft sand, leaving the lights of the city behind. She entered the Valley of the Kings feeling fear and anticipation. It seemed that hours had passed when at last she reached the tomb. She slowly, silently stepped down the stairway leading to the tomb entrance. Then, hearing a sound, she realized she wasn't alone.

Name: _____ Date: _____

Athens & Sparta

Assignment Guidelines

This week you will be working with a partner to produce two storyboards that tell about young people's lives in ancient Athens and Sparta.

1. First research to find out about life in Athens and Sparta.
2. One storyboard will show the life of a Spartan youngster, the other the life of an Athenian youngster.
3. You should have at least four segments in each storyboard (more if you wish).
4. Print information beneath each illustration, explaining what each illustration is showing or adding additional facts.
5. Share your work with the class, showing your storyboards, describing the illustrations, and noting the differences between life in Athens and Sparta.

Illustration	Illustration	Illustration	Illustration
This picture shows me standing in the marketplace of Agora. Merchants come from all over the world with goods to sell.	This picture shows my family and me meeting with other families in the Acropolis. We gather there sometimes.	This shows a great statue of a goddess.	This shows a very great battle that my people fought with the Persians.

Life of a Twelve-year-old in Ancient Athens

Writing Myths

Assignment Guidelines

A **myth** is a legendary story that is usually concerned with deities or demigods and the creation of the world and its inhabitants. Myths were written by several ancient cultures (most notably the Greeks,

Romans, and Norse) as a way to explain the world around them when they did not have scientific explanations for happenings. This week you will be writing a myth. Your assignment for the week is:

1. After you are familiar with myths, begin developing a plan for your own myth. You may use any style of planning (a story web, storyboard, outline, or lists of events), but you must plan in some way.
2. After planning, begin writing your first draft, keeping in mind the following:
   a. Myths were stories that people made up to explain nature or an occurrence that was not easily understood.
   b. These stories involved the gods of the people.
   c. The gods were sometimes mischievous or not kind to the humans.
3. Write your final draft and mount it on a piece of poster board.
4. Place at least two hand-drawn and colored illustrations on the poster.
5. Prepare a presentation for the class, telling the basic story you have written, but not reading the entire story.

Sample Myth Ideas

1. A talkative village would not let the goddess Athena speak at the dinner party held for her, because they were so proud of their own words and did not want to hear words from any others, even a goddess. Athena became so angry she changed the villagers into crickets and now they must chirp incessantly.
2. The god Zeus decided to visit the earth for a holiday. In those days, trees floated above the earth and wandered wherever they desired, so the trees danced for Zeus. The third year he came for the holiday the trees became bored and fell asleep. The great god Zeus became so enraged that he bound the trees to the earth, not allowing them to dance any longer.
3. There was once a red flower that bloomed all year long. One day as the goddess Venus wandered through the gardens, the red flower whispered to its sister that not even Venus could compare with their own beauty. Because Venus was a goddess, she could hear all things. When she heard what the flower said, she condemned them to bloom only in the deepest winter.

Name: _____ Date: _____

Ancient Greece & Rome

Assignment Guidelines

This week you will be researching the ancient empires of Greece and Rome. Use any available resources to find information on these two great civilizations. After researching, you will transfer your information to a poster similar to the layout shown below. This is your assignment for the week:

1. You will work with a partner or in a cooperative learning group.
2. Research ancient Greece and Rome, finding as much information as you can about each empire in these categories:
   a. The form of government
   b. The form of military training
   c. The actual land held by each country at their peak
   d. The homes and living styles
   e. The clothing the people wore
3. After you have gathered the information, condense it so it will fit on the poster.
4. Print the information on the poster and add illustrations.

Greece-Rome Comparison Chart

Characteristics	Greece	Rome
Government		
Military		
Land Held	Map	Map
Living		
Clothing		

Name: _____   Date: _____

A Manor Newspaper

Assignment Guidelines

This week you will be producing one page for a newspaper written in the Middle Ages that might have been delivered to the persons living on a manor and to those in surrounding manors. Your assignment is as follows:

1. Research life on manors during the Middle Ages.
2. Working as a group, compose one page of a manor newspaper.
3. Each person in the group will be responsible for writing one article about the manor or about people living on the manor.
4. Each article should be completely edited and revised.
5. The perfected draft should then be copied in pen into strips of paper as wide as a column on your page.
6. After everyone has copied their articles, arrange them carefully on the page before gluing them down.
7. Add headlines and two or three drawings on the page to go along with the articles.

Suggestions for Articles

1. An article about a person who works at a craft; for example, a cooper, mason, or carpenter

2. An announcement from the king to his people

3. An announcement and advertisement for an upcoming festival

4. A warning about attacks by lawless thieves on the nearby manors

5. An announcement and biography about the manor's newest knight

Moravian Herald

Celebration to be Held at Manor

Hear Ye, Hear Ye, the King himself has news for his people.

The great harvest this season has warranted a feast. It is declared that the thirtieth day of the month will see great celebration. All are invited to the manor this day.

Meet Sir Percival

Newly appointed knight to his majesty, Sir Percival hails from the south of France.

Sir Percival is skilled in all manner of weaponry, including broadsword and the lance. He welcomes the chance to display his talents at the next joust.

Name: _____ Date: _____

A Knight's Story

Assignment Guidelines

This week you will be studying how knights were trained in the Middle Ages and writing a story that tells how a young boy becomes a knight. You will hand in the following items:

1. Write sketches of three characters for your story. For example, you could choose a young knight in training, the knight who is assigned to train him, a young woman who lives in the manor house where the knight is trained, or the lord and owner of the manor.
2. Write the first draft of a story that incorporates the steps of becoming a knight (page, squire, knight). This story will be a fictional piece about a person who is in training for knighthood. Edit and revise the draft.
3. Rewrite or type the final draft of your story.
4. Do a full-color illustration of your knight, complete with armor and weapons.
5. Make a picture of the coat of arms that the knight will bear on his shield.

Suggestions for Story Lines

There once was a very poor but very brave young boy who was the son of a lowly serf on the manor named Harrowsmithe. The boy's name was William, and each day he followed his father into the fields to till the soil. At night when he lay in bed, he dreamed of becoming a knight just like Sir Lawrence, who spoke to William each time he passed by. William also dreamed of marrying the daughter of the lord of the manor. He had seen her at a festival on Saint Benedict's Day. Her name was Elizabeth.

Christopher arrived at the castle one night dripping wet from the rain that had fallen for many days. He was wet, muddy, and miserable after leaving his family and coming with his father to this cold, lonely place. His father had committed him to the lord of the castle when he was born, and now his training for knighthood would begin. When the massive doors swung open, there in front of them was a huge man dressed in furs and heavy robes. His father knelt and tugged on Christopher's cloak to do the same. They were hastened into the large hall where a warm fire burned in the great fireplace. The lord quickly called the servants and the sodden pair were brought dry clothing and seated at a long table to be fed. Finally, a tall bearded fellow entered, and Christopher was told that this would be his teacher for the coming years. His name was Sir Walter of Walesborough. He whisked Christopher up off the chair and onto his shoulder.

Name: _____ Date: _____

A Knight in Shining Armor

Assignment Guidelines

For this week's writing, you will first have to obtain information about the feudal system and also find out what part the manor house played in the system. After you have finished researching, you will do the following assignments:

1. Do a time line of the story you are planning. The story must take place on or near a manor house and must involve persons living on the manor. You may also include people who do not live on the manor in your story.
2. After you have planned a time line, write the first draft of the story.
3. When you have completed the first draft and completely edited and revised the copy, write the final draft.
4. Be prepared to share your story by explaining it from the time line, not by reading it from your written copy.

Sample plan for a story in a time line format (Your time line should be more detailed.)

Richard becomes a knight in 1567.	A group of robbers threaten the manor house.	The robbers break into the manor house and steal Princess Leticia.	Sir Richard goes to find Leticia, but meets the thieves, who wound him.	Leticia escapes, finds Richard, nurses him to health and returns to marry him.

Story Ideas

1. The story begins when the entire manor house in Sheffield is filled with guests because a wild boar hunt will take place on the morrow. There is much eating and dancing. The knights have been vigilant as they guard the house from marauders and thieves. The youngest knight, Sir Gerald, is shivering as he stands beneath the torches at the gate. Suddenly he hears a sound in the bushes.
2. Wilfred, the lord's advisor, is an evil man. He has secretly been stealing money from the lord's purse and is planning to murder the lord as he sleeps. Princess Dora hates Wilfred and suspects him of wrongdoing, but her father, the lord, pays no attention to her in this matter. She decides to spy on Wilfred, so she feigns sleep one night, dresses in dark clothing, and sneaks down to the chambers belonging to the malicious Wilfred. She puts her ear to his door to listen.

Name: _____ Date: _____

Renaissance Biographies

Assignment Guidelines

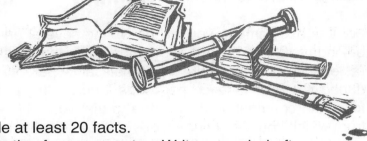

1. Choose a person from the Renaissance to learn more about.
2. Gather information from your sources about the person you have chosen. Record the information on index cards. Include at least 20 facts.
3. Write a biography using the information from your notes. Write a rough draft. Then have another student edit your work. Write the final draft.
4. Include two illustrations and one cover illustration. These are to be full-color drawings.
5. Include a bibliography with your final draft.
6. Prepare and deliver a ten-minute presentation for the class about your person. Do not read directly from your paper.
7. Your evaluation will include:
    a. Your research notes
    b. The thoroughness of your paper
    c. The quality of your presentation
    d. The quality of illustrations

About the Renaissance

The **Renaissance** was a period of history between 1350 and 1650, during which there was significant achievement and change. It was a time that encompassed changes in religion, the growth of nation-states, exploration, and extraordinary accomplishments in the arts, sciences and academic areas. It marked the end of feudalism and the beginning of national governments and the importance of the individual.

The following is a list of a few of the important people who lived during the Renaissance. You may choose another influential person of this time period as long as you obtain your teacher's permission.

• Leonardo da Vinci	• Martin Luther	• Joan of Arc
• Queen Elizabeth I	• Botticelli	• Sir Walter Raleigh
• Alrecht Durer	• Vasco da Gama	• Maximillian
• Michelangelo Buonarotti	• Henry VIII	• William Shakespeare
• Isaac Newton	• Galileo Galilei	• Sir Francis Drake
• Amerigo Vespucci	• Nicholas Copernicus	• Ferdinand Magellan

Name: _____   Date: _____

Renaissance Diaries

Assignment Guidelines

For this assignment, you will be writing several entries in a personal journal or diary that belongs to a person who lived during the Renaissance period. You will write these entries (at least four) as if you are the Renaissance person. You may choose any person who lived during the Renaissance period as long as this person is well-known for some contribution they made to the world. Here are a few names from which you may choose, or you may select your own Renaissance person.

- Leonardo da Vinci
- Nicholas Copernicus
- Michelangelo Buonarotti
- Galileo Galilei
- William Shakespeare
- Isaac Newton
- Chaucer
- Donatello
- Johann Gutenberg
- Joan of Arc
- Christopher Columbus

Example of Diary Entries

This is written as if it is the diary belonging to Michelangelo Buonarotti:

May 15, 1502 – *In painting class today, Signor Ghirlandaio insisted I become a painter for the great house of the Medici Family. I became very angry, for he knows my true passion is for the art of sculpture. I threw my palette and brushes at him. I am going off to sculpt.*

October 25, 1502 – *Since I left painting school, I have been living in my wretched flat on the Tiber River. I must wear gloves, for my hands become numb as I work with the chisel and mallet forming magnificent forms from the wondrous marble. I have little to eat, but once a day Signor Antonio has pity on me and brings me hot soup.*

November 12, 1512 – *I have just found out that the paintings on the ceiling of the Sistine Chapel must end because of money problems. At least it has helped me to survive for the past four years. Now I will go back to my beloved sculpture. In my dreams, many images have come to me of figures I must sculpt!*

Art of the Renaissance

Assignment Guidelines

Your assignment this week will be to thoroughly study the artist who has been assigned to you. Then you will pretend to be this person as you complete the three elements of this assignment. You (the artist) have been asked to submit a resumé and artwork and to appear for an interview with the Medici family, one of the most powerful and wealthy families in Italy.

1. You will study and take notes, listing the accomplishments of your assigned artist.
2. Then develop a resumé. A resumé is a list of your education, the jobs you have held, and your notable accomplishments.
3. Develop a collection of your artwork to present to the Medicis at the interview. You will have to make some drawings to reflect the work of your artist. You can make a folder in which to place the artwork.
4. Finally, act out the interview. One of your classmates will impersonate the interviewing member of the Medici family.

Sample Resumé of a Fictitious Artist

Resumé of **Hernando De La Castile**
Currently of the house of Stabardo in Rome, Italy

Birth date: December 7, 1484

Education: Studied in the house of Bertolucci, Milan, Italy, in the years from 1492 until employed in the house of Stabardo in 1502
Studied fresco painting under Bertolucci
Studied marble sculpture with Michelangelo Buonarotti (1495–1501)
Studied architectural drawing under Leonardo da Vinci (1493–1497)

Accomplishments: Received the Golden Cross for design and creation of the Bertolucci family vault that stands on their estate in Milan

Name: _____   Date: _____

Christopher Columbus Calls for Adventurers

Assignment Guidelines

Your assignment is to design and write a brochure. This brochure will be written as if Christopher Columbus had written it. In this brochure, he will be requesting volunteers to accompany him on his second voyage to the New World. In the writing that you do, it will be important to include the following items so your brochure will be certain to bring you the help that you need:

1. Tell them about yourself (Christopher Columbus) and your experiences as an explorer and competent sailor.
2. Tell of the wonderful adventures people will experience if they accompany you.
3. Tell of the breathtaking new land that they will see when they arrive in the New World.
4. Tell about the possibility of gold and riches they may find and anything else that will tempt them to go with you.
5. List the necessary characteristics the fellow adventurers must have as they embark on this journey.
6. The illustrations and decorations on your brochure will be in color, and the writing should be in black ink.

Designing Your Brochure

1. Get a large piece of white art paper.

2. Place the paper horizontally.

3. Using a ruler, divide the paper in three sections.

4. Fold the two side sections inward. Print your copy on the six sections of the brochure. Be sure to edit and revise your work carefully.

5. The front of your brochure should have a full-color illustration. The other five sides should have printing and a smaller illustration on each page.

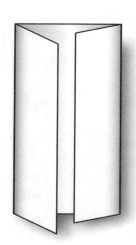

Name: _____ Date: _____

Great Explorers

Assignment Guidelines

This week you will be reading about the great explorers. These men came from many lands and navigated the seven seas, discovering new routes and establishing trade. You will choose one of these men and study what his accomplishments were. A list of these explorers is given below, and the following are the requirements for this assignment.

1. First read all that you can about this person.
2. As you research, take notes on the explorer, being sure to include interesting facts about the many explorations he made.
3. Write a **monologue** (a speech given alone), pretending that you are the explorer. You have just returned from an extensive voyage and have been invited to speak before a large crowd of merchants who are interested in donating money for your next trip. You have to convince them that you have a worthy cause and that they would be wise to invest in your next exploration.
4. After you write your speech, present it to the class.
5. You may use costumes (gathered from the things you have at home), and you can include maps, charts, and hand-drawn pictures of things you may have seen in your travels.

Great Explorers

- Vasco da Gama
- Bartholomew Dias
- Ferdinand Magellan
- Francisco Coronado
- Prince Henry the Navigator
- Henry Hudson
- Sir Walter Raleigh
- Jacques Marquette
- Vasco Nunez de Balboa

- Eric the Red
- Amerigo Vespucci
- Hernando Cortez
- Francisco Pizarro
- John Cabot
- Jacques Cartier
- Samuel de Champlain
- Giovanni de Verrazano
- Bjarni Herjulfsson

- Leif Ericson
- Marco Polo
- Hernando de Soto
- Junipero Serra
- Christopher Columbus
- Sir Francis Drake
- Louis Joliet
- Juan Ponce de Leon

Name: _____ Date: _____

Native North Americans

Assignment Guidelines

Before Europeans landed on the North American continent, there were many groups of people that were scattered all across the land, each with different customs and ways of dealing with their physical environment. For this week's lesson, you will be researching three Native American tribes. Your assignments are as follows:

1. Find out the following information about the three tribes you select:
   a. Where they lived
   b. What kind of houses they built
   c. What kind of clothing they wore
   d. How they supported and fed themselves
   e. How they governed themselves
2. Research, take notes, and gather pictures to place on a piece of poster board as shown below.
3. Share the information on the poster with the class.

A Partial List of Tribes

- Pueblo
- Iroquois
- Cherokee
- Eastern Woodland
- Chickasaw
- Sioux
- Seminole
- Creek
- Powhatan
- Susquehanna
- Chumash
- Algonquian
- Apache
- Blackfoot
- Navajo

Comparing Native American Tribes			
	Sioux	**Cree**	**Powhatan**
Location			
House			
Clothing			
Food			
Government			
Other information			

Name: _____ Date: _____

The First Thanksgiving

Assignment Guidelines

This week you will write a story about the first Thanksgiving feast. This is your assignment:

1. Read the information below about the Pilgrims from the book *The American Nation* by Garraty and McCaughey. Gather information from other sources if needed.
2. Choose a character who would have been a part of the first Thanksgiving.
3. Decide where you will start your story—on the *Mayflower*, on the shore, at the festivities after the meal, or some other place.
4. Write a story about the first Thanksgiving from this character's perspective.

The Pilgrims were a religious group, also known as the Puritans, who were not happy with the Anglican Church in England. They fled to Holland in 1608, led by three men: their pastor, John Robinson; William Brewster, a church elder; and William Bradford. By 1619, they were again disheartened because they could not make a living, because others of their church in England would not come to Holland, and because their children were being influenced by children who were not of their faith. Therefore, about 100 Pilgrims made arrangements to sail to the New World on the *Mayflower* in September 1620. They arrived in Cape Cod Bay in December of the same year. It was a cold and snowy area, but they decided to stay rather than venture out into the stormy sea once again.

They chose William Bradford to be their new governor. That first winter proved to be very harsh and about half of them perished from hunger. They met a Native American man named Squanto who befriended them and showed them good places to fish and hunt. He also helped them plant their crops and served as an interpreter. The Pilgrims began working very hard and were rewarded with a wonderful harvest the following fall. To show their gratitude to their Native American friends, they invited them to the first Thanksgiving feast, which we still celebrate in America today.

Example Characters

1. You are a child. Your parents have decided to come to the New World, but you are frightened as you embark on this new journey.

2. You are a mother of three small children. You have come to the New World with your husband, church elder William Brewster. He is a stern man. One frigid February, William opens the door of the cabin. You are astonished to see a tall, dark-skinned man dressed in fur and leather standing at the door.

3. You are a young child whose ancestors have lived on the shores of Cape Cod for generations. You have heard about these new white settlers, but still you stand in awe as you view their huge ship approaching.

A Colonial Newspaper

Assignment Guidelines

This week you will be writing articles for one of the first colonial newspapers and producing the front page of the newspaper. You may call your newspaper anything you wish and use any headlines that you think would have been appropriate for such a paper. Be sure to include dates and places that would be realistic. The following is a list of your guidelines for the week:

1. Research life in the colonies.
2. One part of your newspaper page will be an interview with a new immigrant. You will interview another classmate who will pretend to be a colonist who has recently come to the New World. After you interview your partner, your partner will interview you as you pretend to be another colonist who will be featured in another article. Before your interview, write down the questions you will ask. Leave space between the questions so you will have room to write the answers.
3. Use your notes from the interview to write an article about this person.
4. Other articles on the page should reflect news and happenings that would likely be reported in a colonial newspaper.
5. Copy the articles onto a large sheet of paper. Add headlines and pictures.

The Plymouth Times

Colonists Pour Into the Area!

This interview was given by Priscilla Mullins on January 5, 1635, in her home on the shore of Boston Harbor. She lives there with her husband and two sons, Daniel and Charles. Her mother and father also live in their cabin. The Mullins family came here two years ago.

Name: _____ Date: _____

Colonial Life Play

Assignment Guidelines

This week you will write a play that takes place in a colonial cabin or house. Here are some guidelines to follow as you begin your writing:

1. You will work in a group to write and perform a play about life in colonial America.
2. Have each person in your group research a different source to find information about what life was like for the colonists. Combine the information and incorporate it in your play.
3. Write a script and hand in a copy to your teacher the day of the performance.
4. Each person in the group must have a speaking part, but a person may play more than one character if you need more characters than the number of people in your group.
5. Each day this week, one person of each group will work on creating the backdrop for the plays.
6. If you wish, you may gather props and simple costumes that will make your play more exciting.
7. You will be evaluated on the effort you put forth, your cooperation in the group, and on your final performance.

Suggestions for Plots

1. A stranger stops by your cabin for a cool drink and tells you that he heard there have been a rash of attacks on colonists by a small band of robbers. He heard they are only a few days' ride from your village.
2. You woke up this morning to find your three-year-old son missing from the cabin.
3. You are sitting in your house late at night having a cup of tea when you hear a groan outside the door.
4. Your nearest neighbor is about a half mile away and you wake up one morning very ill with a fever. There are only you and your twin girls who are eight years old in the cabin. Suddenly, there is a knock at the door.

Name: _____ Date: _____

Come to the Colonies

Assignment Guidelines

This week you will be designing a travel poster that will be distributed throughout Europe in the middle 1600s or early 1700s. Here are your guidelines for the project:

1. Choose a colony and research the colony. Take notes on things you find appealing about the colony or that someone else might find appealing about this place.
2. Pretend you are living in this colony and you have the job of making a travel poster to entice Europeans to settle in the colony.
3. On this travel poster you must include several things:
   a. An attention-getting title
   b. A summary of great things to see in the colony
   c. A paragraph that would make people want to come to your colony
   d. Several small illustrations showing things about the colony
   e. Information about a house that is available for rent or sale
4. Prepare a presentation to share with the class.

Colonies

The following is a list of the colonies that you may choose or your teacher will assign one to you:

- Jamestown
- Plymouth
- New Haven
- New Sweden
- New Netherland
- Fort Orange
- New Amsterdam
- Fort Christina
- St. Mary's
- Boston
- Salem
- Portsmouth
- St. Augustine
- Williamsburg

Come Live in Jamestown

The air is fresh.
The water is clean.
Come for adventure.
Leave city life behind!
Come, begin anew in a
beautiful, rich land!

The Revolution Begins

Assignment Guidelines: Day One

This week you will be writing about the events leading to the Revolutionary War. There are two acts that were passed in England that subjected the colonists to high taxes. These acts were the **Townsend Act** and the **Stamp Act**. Read about these acts. Then do the following:

1. Explain each of the two laws, telling what items were taxed by each law.
2. Tell why the British imposed these acts.
3. Give your own opinion of these taxes and tell what you would have done if you were a colonist and had to pay the taxes.

Day Two

Today you will be reading about the reaction the colonists had to the British taxes. Read about these people and events and then write answers to the questions that follow.

- The Sons of Liberty
- The Boston Massacre
- Patrick Henry's speech
- The Boston Tea Party

1. Explain how and why the Sons of Liberty formed and who some of the members were.
2. Who was Patrick Henry and why did he make his famous speech?
3. What happened at the Boston Massacre and what was the result of this?
4. What was the Boston Tea Party, why did it occur, and who was involved?
5. Make a time line of these important events plus any other important related events between 1765 and 1776.

Day Three

Choose three people or groups from the list below and write short reports on index cards (one person/group per card). Using a transparency or a class whiteboard, list two or three main points about each of the people/groups. Share this information with the class.

- John Adams
- Paul Revere
- Thomas Paine
- Robert Livingston
- Samuel Adams
- Thomas Jefferson
- Richard Henry Lee
- The Hessians
- John Dickinson
- John Hancock
- Benjamin Franklin

Day Four

Pretend you are living in the time right before the Revolutionary War and write your story. Use actual events that occurred in that period. Here are a few suggestions.

1. You are a newspaper person covering the volatile events in your city.
2. You are a young person living in Boston. Your mother has just sent you to the market. Suddenly British troops come rushing into the street.
3. You are a member of the Sons of Liberty. It is night. There's a knock on your door.
4. You are a young British soldier who has been assigned to guard the angry crowd in the Boston marketplace.

Name: _____ Date: _____

Reporting on the Revolution

Assignment Guidelines

This week you will be working in a group and will be learning about the battles that were fought during the Revolutionary War. After you research the battles your teacher assigns, you will develop a script for a news show that you will deliver on the last day of this unit.

1. Research the Revolutionary War battle that your teacher assigned to your group.
2. Decide on the format for your news show. For example:
   a. An anchor news person could announce the battle that is being covered and other persons in the group could portray a reporter who is covering the battle and participants in the battle.
   b. You could begin directly from the battleground, having reporters interviewing generals and soldiers.
3. Write the first draft of your show. It should include the facts about the battle, as well as commentary or opinion. It does not matter who gives the facts and opinions, but it is necessary that both are given.
4. Make a map to show the location of the battle and its relationship to other battles.
5. Write a final draft, memorize the parts, and present your newscast.

Sample Script

Reporter: Here we are at Valley Forge, the scene of the Continental Army's winter camp for 1777–78. General Washington has held the troops together through the bitterly cold winter. The Continental Army has suffered severe supply shortages. Here is Martha Washington now. She is bringing food to those recovering from injuries. Mrs. Washington, could we take a few moments of your time?

Mrs. Washington: Of course, but I have much to do.

Reporter: Mrs. Washington, why are you here in this cold uninviting place?

Mrs. Washington: Well, I have come to assist in any way I can. There are many women who are involved in the war, not directly in battle, but tending the wounded, cooking, preparing bandages, and many other duties. I feel that I must also do my part.

Reporter: Thank you so much for speaking with us. Here is General Washington. General, why is there such a shortage of supplies?

Name: _____ Date: _____

Life After the Revolutionary War

Assignment Guidelines

This week you will pretend that you are living in the colonies following the Revolutionary War. You have a friend who is in Europe and you are keeping in touch with your friend by writing letters. You are anxious to tell your friend all that is going on. The following is your assignment for the week:

1. You will write at least three or more letters to your imaginary friend.
2. Each of these letters must make reference to actual events that happened in the period after the war.
3. You may need to do additional research to make your writing more exciting.
4. Include details in your writing about your daily life, as well as the political climate.
5. Include your feelings about the new country, your hopes for the future, and your fears.

Facts About the Period Following the War

1. The Articles of Confederation were adopted as the first governmental plan approved by the Continental Congress.
2. In 1787, the Northwest Ordinance was passed, which divided the Northwest into smaller territories. The people in these territories had the same rights as other Americans. No slavery was permitted in these areas.
3. By 1787, the states were arguing about boundaries, trade, taxes, and money (each state used different currency, and one state would not accept another state's money).
4. To settle these disputes, the states sent a total of 55 delegates to Philadelphia.
5. The delegates decided to change the current system of government and develop a constitution instead of the Articles of Confederation.
6. An agreement called the Great Compromise determined that there would be two houses in Congress, the House of Representatives and the Senate.

Sample Letter

Dearest Margaret,

So much has happened. Here at Mount Vernon we have been busy with the year's harvest. George had hoped he could retire and settle down to a long life as a gentleman farmer, but they have chosen him as a delegate of this great new state (no longer a colony) of Virginia. I cannot say that I am not proud, but he has done so much already for this new land, and I know he wishes it could be otherwise. He feels such a strong sense of duty. I knew this when I married him, and my love grows for him each and every day.

Yours truly,

Martha

Name: _____ Date: _____

Studying the Constitution

Premise

A citizen's group has decided that we should change the way our government is organized. You have been chosen to defend one of the branches of government (judicial, executive, or legislative) in a public debate that will inform people as to whether they should vote for the referendum to change the government. If you are convincing, the voters will decide to keep the government as it is now. If you are not convincing, the citizens may vote to change the Constitution and the way our government is organized. You must research thoroughly and plan your defenses expertly.

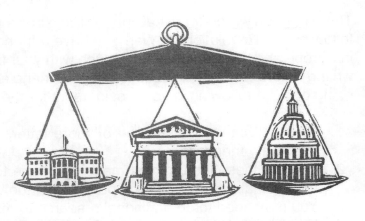

Assignment Guidelines

This week you will work with a group to prepare a defense of the branch of government that you have been assigned. As you work, be sure to include all the following parts in your defense:

1. The first day should be spent researching the branch of government you are assigned. Divide the research tasks up equally among the members of the group. Try to find the following information about the branch:
   a. The positions that make up the branch: list each one and tell how the people are chosen
   b. The specific duties of the persons in the branch (if this branch is a group, list their general and specific duties)
   c. How this branch works with the other branches or balances the other branches
   d. Why you think it is necessary to keep this branch
2. Write a commentary about how this branch has worked in the past. Give examples of what would happen if this branch did not exist. Tell why it is necessary to keep this branch of government.
3. Write an outline for your group's presentation and decide who will say what. All members must have a speaking part in the defense.
4. Finally, write your speeches, memorize and practice them. Encourage passionate performances from each member of the group. It may be effective if you accompany your speech with charts, diagrams, transparencies, or other presentation aids.

Name: _____ Date: _____

The Bill of Rights

Assignment Guidelines

This week in class you will be studying our country's Bill of Rights. You will think about: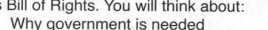

- Why government is needed
- How one would go about writing a plan for a country

Day One

You will be working with a small group to develop a short skit showing one of the following situations:

1. What would happen in an imaginary country that has no government at all; no laws, no law enforcers, or judges?
2. What would happen in a country that has rules and laws but no law enforcers?
3. What would happen in a country that has rules and laws and law enforcers but no one to settle disputes (like courts)?

Present a problem, try to settle it in some way, and show what happens when no decision can be reached.

Day Two

Today you will read the Bill of Rights. After you read this material, work with your group to do the following:

1. Pretend that your group has been selected to rewrite the Bill of Rights.
2. Discuss the rights you think should be rewritten, the ones you think should be eliminated, and new rights that should be added.
3. Create a Bill of Rights by writing first a working copy and then copying the final draft onto large chart paper.
4. Discuss the consequences of each right. Be prepared to share your reasoning for including the rights you have chosen.

Day Three

Today you will read about different types of national governments that exist in the countries below. List the characteristics of each government on chart paper. Be prepared to share your findings.

- Cuba
- France
- England
- India
- Israel
- Argentina
- Brazil
- Iraq
- Iran

Day Four

Today you will think about the citizens of a country and their responsibilities to the government. Discuss this with your group. After your discussion, each person should write a short paper listing the responsibilities he or she thinks every citizen should accept. Some examples might be:

- Pay taxes
- Obey the laws
- Help the police
- Serve on a jury

Name: _____ Date: _____

The Haunting of Monticello

Assignment Guidelines

For this project, you will begin by doing research about the life of Thomas Jefferson, his wife Martha, their children, and their home, Monticello, in Virginia. The following is a list of your assignments:

1. You will be writing a story about Thomas Jefferson and his daughters living at Monticello.
2. In the story, you must have one or more ghosts. The ghost could be a historical figure or someone from Jefferson's personal life, like his wife, who died at age 33, or one of Jefferson's other children, who died either at birth or at a young age.
3. Your story can have fact mixed with fiction. For example, you could have Benjamin Franklin coming each night to give Thomas Jefferson advice when Jefferson serves as president of the United States or ambassador to France.
4. When you have researched the idea, write a first draft, revise, and edit carefully. Then make a final draft, inserting illustrations throughout the story.
5. Make a cover for your story.

Facts to Inspire Your Writing

Thomas Jefferson's first structure at Monticello was called "the Little House," because it was just one room measuring 18 feet by 18 feet. This is the house he brought his wife to in the winter of 1772.

Thomas met Martha in 1770 and a little more than a year later, on New Year's Day of 1772, he married her. On their wedding day, there was a severe snowstorm that made travel impossible. Two weeks later, they began the 100-mile journey to Monticello through deep snow. When they arrived, it was late, the servants were asleep, and the food was cold. They sat by candlelight, whispering and giggling until very late.

Ten years later, after the birth of her last child, Martha died. Thomas stayed locked in his room for three weeks. The servants feared that he too would die. He never fully recovered from the loss of his wife, and he never married again. He went on to serve his country as ambassador, secretary of state, vice president, and president. He died in 1826.

Name: _____ Date: _____

American Industry & Transportation

Assignment Guidelines

An **industrial revolution** is a time during a country's history when there is rapid change from a farming to an industrial society. The Industrial Revolution began in Britain in the late 18th and early 19th centuries. The innovations from Britain quickly spread to the United States.

This week, you will be finding out about the way the United States expanded industrially during the time between the Revolutionary War and the Civil War. Below are the research choices and some ideas for the project. This is what you will do:

1. Select a topic and research and write a paper on the topic you choose.
   a. Gather information on your topic and record it on index cards. Get enough information to fill five or more cards.
   b. Make an outline of the information. It must be clear, concise and interesting.
   c. Write a rough draft.
   d. Edit your work and write a final draft that is typed or neatly written.
   e. Include a bibliography listing all your resources.
2. Construct a model or make a drawing of the object of your research.
3. Finally, present your findings and your project to the entire class.

Research Choices

- Locomotive
- Cash register
- Steamboat
- Conestoga wagon
- Sewing machine
- Clipper ship
- Powered loom
- Telegraph
- Reaper
- Elevator
- Suspension bridge
- Cotton gin
- The Erie Canal
- Stagecoach
- Franklin stove
- Spinning jenny
- Flying shuttle
- Steam engine
- Rubber
- Steel plow
- Bicycle
- First American factory

Project Ideas

You should choose a project that will clearly show other people how the object you researched functioned. Some ideas for projects include:

- Diorama
- Poster
- Scale model
- Diagram

The Abolition Movement

Assignment Guidelines

This week, you will be learning about the movement to abolish slavery in America. Working with a partner, you will research one of the terms listed below. Then you will write a skit or presentation involving the person(s) or subject.

1. Research the topic you are assigned.
2. Write a skit, debate, sermon, mock trial, panel discussion, or presentation telling about the person or event, how this affected the institution of slavery, and how it contributed to the Civil War.
3. Make your presentation to class.

Sample Topics

- American Anti-Slavery Society
- Underground Railroad
- William Lloyd Garrison
- Harriet Beecher Stowe & *Uncle Tom's Cabin*
- Frederick Douglass
- Harriet Tubman
- Sarah & Angelina Grimke
- Sojourner Truth
- Compromise of 1850
- Kansas-Nebraska Act
- "Bleeding Kansas"
- The Lincoln-Douglas Debates
- John Brown's Raid on Harper's Ferry
- 13th Amendment

Presentation Ideas

Here are some ideas for presentations.

1. You could portray two people traveling north on the Underground Railroad. The skit could begin in the basement of a home in Virginia as the two enslaved persons speak about the dangers they have experienced on their journey.
2. If you are portraying a famous person, you may want to pretend that you have been asked to speak to a group of people about your beliefs and accomplishments. Pretend you are on stage in a small hall in New York or Philadelphia.
3. You could be a professor in a university teaching about the topic you were assigned.
4. You could pretend that you have been called to argue about the topic in a public place.
5. You could choose to interview the person, asking their opinions on different issues.
6. If you are presenting a law or debate, you can present both sides of the argument in a reenactment of the debate.

The Civil War Explodes

Assignment Guidelines

This project will last two weeks and will include the following four projects.

1. Make a time line of Civil War events. If time permits, add illustrations.
2. You will be assigned a famous person. Find out what clothing was worn at the time and create a picture of this person in full dress. Underneath the figure, you will write a short synopsis of his or her life on an index card.
3. You will be assigned a famous battle or event. On a square piece of paper, write a title, make an illustration, map, or symbol of the event and write a short statement of why it was important. Your square will be hung with other squares as a part of the class Civil War quilt.
4. Construct a game board and question cards to go with the board. Include a wide range of questions that cover the events leading to the war, those during the war, and those immediately following the Civil War.

Famous People

- Abraham Lincoln
- General Ulysses S. Grant
- General Robert E. Lee
- Stonewall Jackson
- Jefferson Davis
- John Brown
- Winfield Scott
- Belle Boyd
- General George McClellan
- Clara Barton
- General George Pickett
- General William T. Sherman

Important Events

- Missouri Compromise
- Compromise of 1850
- Uncle Tom's Cabin published
- Kansas-Nebraska Act
- Dred Scott Decision
- Election of 1860
- Confederate States Secede from Union
- Emancipation Proclamation
- Trent Affair
- Appomattox Surrender
- Assassination of Lincoln

Famous Battles

- Fort Sumter
- Bull Run
- Vicksburg
- Antietam
- Gettysburg
- Fredericksburg
- Appomattox
- Mobile Bay
- Atlanta
- Shiloh
- Vicksburg
- Chattanooga
- The Wilderness
- New Orleans

Name: _____ Date: _____

Civil War Journals

Assignment Guidelines

This week, you will be pretending that you are an enlisted man in the Civil War fighting for the North or the South and writing several entries in a journal or diary. Because the journal must tell about at least one specific battle of the war, it will be necessary for you to have good references.

1. Your journal should contain at least four entries.
2. Write the diary as if you are a soldier and you want to leave your loved ones a memento of your experiences, or write the journal as if you are a correspondent for a newspaper during the war, and your newspaper is going to print the journal as a feature in one of the issues.
3. Include the following information:
   a. Tell about the members of your family and where you live. This can be totally fictional.
   b. Tell about your experiences in the war so far. This can be a combination of actual events and fiction.
   c. Explain the battle you are fighting in at the moment. This part should be fairly factual but passionate and full of description.
   d. Finally, describe your commanding officer, telling what kind of commander he is and what he is most probably thinking and feeling.
   e. If you are writing as a newspaper correspondent, write what you observe the soldiers and the commanders around you doing, what your feelings about the battle are, and any conversations you have with the other men.

Sample Entry

July 20, 1861

I know that I may never see my loved ones again, but I wanted to write this journal as my only legacy to them from a war that is just beginning.

It is night and I sit beneath a tree at Manassas Junction. We are gathered about our campfire, a banjo playing a soft tune. From the rumors among the men, we will attack tomorrow. I am hopeful that this will be a brief war. The northern states must see that we are deserving of our independence. General Beauregard, our commanding officer, is an arrogant leader, sure of winning. I hope that he is right.

I am thinking of my loved ones at home in our humble dwelling. My smallest child is just one year old, about to walk. Amelia has light hair the color of flax and cheeks as rosy as a summer's day. My oldest child, Thomas, is full of spirit and curiosity. He is ten years of age. When I think there is a possibility of never seeing them again, I am filled with sorrow.

Name: _____ Date: _____

Civil War Battles

Assignment Guidelines

For your project this week, you will be working in groups to accomplish your task. You will be assigned a particular battle of the Civil War. You will portray the battle on a large mural with the characters that participated in it and the scenery surrounding the area. The following is a list of guidelines for your work this week:

1. After you have been assigned a battle, begin researching the battle. You will need to find the following facts:
   a. Where and when the battle took place
   b. The major characters or officers of the battle
   c. What the terrain was like
   d. A chronological list of the actual events of the battle
2. Copy all of your information onto large index cards in an orderly manner or print it out on the computer.
3. Draw and color a picture of the battle, and glue the information from your research on the mural.

Some Battles of the Civil War

- Bull Run – Manassas, VA
- Antietam in Maryland
- Vicksburg, Mississippi
- Fredericksburg in Virginia
- Shiloh in Tennessee
- Fort Sumter – Charleston, SC
- Chancellorsville, Virginia
- Sherman's March to the Sea
- Gettysburg, Pennsylvania
- Atlanta, Georgia

You may choose battles other than these with your teacher's permission.

The Battle of Bull Run/Manassas

When and where did the battle take place?	Important characters	Important events

Name: _____ Date: _____

Speech Writing for President Lincoln

Assignment Guidelines

This week, you will be writing a speech for President Lincoln. This speech will be delivered to a large gathering that has come to see the president sign the Emancipation Proclamation. You will pretend that you have been President Lincoln's friend since boyhood. You have been with him since 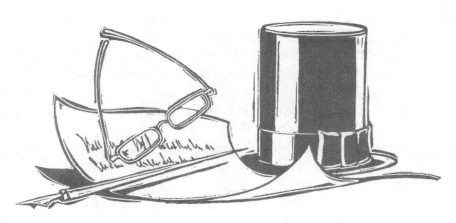 he began traveling the country years ago. You have seen all the things that he has seen—slavery in the South; the buying and selling of enslaved persons who have been abused, underfed, and poorly housed. You, personally, are against slavery, even though you know that southern plantation owners argue that slavery is an economic necessity. You must write a speech that Americans of conflicting beliefs will hear, convincing them that slavery is evil and that it is now ended.

Your assignment, therefore, is to write a speech that President Lincoln will give before or after signing this law. He will tell what the law says, why he signed it into law, the things that he saw as he traveled through the South, and his hopes for the future of all men.

Optional Elements

You will be presenting your speech before the class as if you are Lincoln. Here are some suggestions to make your presentation more dramatic. You do not have to add any of these options.

1. You may wear a costume.

2. You may choose or compose a short piece of music to be played during your speech or following it.

Ideas for Speech Writing

Here is a sample beginning of the speech.

We are gathered here today to witness a great moment. Long has the issue pressed upon my heart, for I have known slavery to be an appalling injustice to our fellow men, women, and children. I would like to tell you some of my experiences with slavery as I have traveled the country in my younger years and after entering the law profession and politics.

Name: _____ Date: _____

Reconstruction

Assignment Guidelines

This week, you will be researching the Reconstruction Period following the Civil War and presenting the information in a talk show format. Your presentation will be to a large audience at a college in Williamsburg, Virginia. Your presentation should tell what life is like in the period of Reconstruction in the South.

1. Research what life would have been like for the persons listed in the box below.
2. Choose several of these characters for your presentation. Do more in-depth research on these people.
3. Assign roles and write a script.
4. Present your show.

List of Characters

- **The Talk Show Host** – This could be one of the college professors or the college president.
- **A Carpetbagger** – A person who has left the North and moved to the South to make a fortune out of the postwar chaos
- **A Confederate Soldier** – A person returning to his farm in the South only to find it has been devastated by the ravages of war
- **An Employee of the Freedman's Bureau** – A person who is working to assist newly-freed enslaved persons with their basic needs
- **Blanche K. Bruce** – A formerly enslaved man who has been well-educated and has political aspirations
- **President Andrew Johnson** – The man who became president after Lincoln's assassination
- **A Sharecropper** – A former enslaved person who has been given a small piece of land to farm with the agreement that he share his production with the landowner

Excerpt of a Sample Script

Host – *Good evening and welcome to a very special discussion. We have here on stage a few guests who would like to share their experiences since the end of the war and the effects the war has had upon their lives. Our first guest is Randolf Hutchinson of Vicksburg, Mississippi. Mr. Hutchinson, tell us of your experience after you returned home.*

Hutchinson – *Well, as you know, I fought with the Confederate Army. When I returned to my farm near Vicksburg, I wept; for my house was burnt to the ground and my family, all dead. As you can imagine, I was in a state of despair.*

Name: _____ Date: _____

The Gold Rush

Assignment Guidelines

For this lesson, you will make a poster about the Gold Rush. First, find out all you can about this period in history. Take notes carefully, concentrating on the following areas:

1. Where the gold mines were located
2. When the Gold Rush and subsequent mining took place
3. The various methods used to obtain gold
4. The hazards of mining gold
5. The effects of the Gold Rush on the development of the West

After completing all your research, begin transferring the information to a poster similar to the poster shown below. Illustrate in any area that you can.

Gold Rush Information

   The **Gold Rush** is a term to describe the rush of prospectors into the remote regions of the West between 1849 and 1915. It started when John Sutter discovered gold at his mill in Sacramento, California, in 1848. The frantic search for gold brought over 80,000 people to California in one year. Only a few of these adventurers found gold. A second gold rush began in Colorado in 1858, and a third rush of miners into the Klondike gold fields took place in 1897.

── Gold Mining Chart ──

A map showing the gold mining areas with the dates of production	The methods used to obtain gold
The hazards of gold mining	The effects that gold mining had on the settlement in the West

Name: _____ Date: _____

The Westward Movement

Assignment Guidelines

For your writing assignment this week, you will be studying and writing about the Western Movement, a movement of settlers to the western part of the United States during the mid-1800s. You will be writing a letter to tell about your decision as to whether to move to the West or stay in the East. This is what you will do:

1. Read the writing situation below.
2. Research conditions in the United States between 1840 and 1870. Find out what motivated people to move west and what hazards they faced when they made the journey west.
3. Decide whether you will move West or stay in the East. Make a list of problems you will face in the place you have decided to live and give the arguments in favor of this decision.
4. Compose a letter to your father explaining your decision. Address all your father's concerns and give convincing reasons for going or staying.

The Western Movement

More than a quarter of a million Americans crossed the continent to the Oregon Territory between 1840 and 1870. To those hopeful emigrants from the East, Oregon seemed to be the promised land with rich soil and abundant resources. Promoters and advocates of the western movement painted a glowing picture of a farmer's paradise. While the East was experiencing a prolonged period of unemployment and falling prices, going West presented its own problems. To reach Oregon, the pioneers had to travel the Oregon Trail—2,000 miles over prairie, desert, and mountains. There were numerable hardships to be faced before people could reach their destination. Many people died or gave up along the way.

Writing Situation

You are a young healthy person who is married and has one child. You live in Missouri, and the year is 1841. You own land and raise corn, but the price of your crop has been dropping. You and your spouse are thinking of moving to Oregon, the "promised land." You must decide whether to stay or go. Once you decide, you must write a letter to your father, telling him about your decision and convincing him that you are making the right decision.

Men of the West

Assignment Guidelines

For this project, you will be writing a newspaper article about one of the men who lived and worked on the western frontier. These were men who shaped the West. The following are the tasks you will complete:

1. Choose one of the men who explored and settled the West and do research on the person. Find out all you can about this famous Westerner that would make an interesting story for readers of a newspaper. Take notes on index cards.
2. Pretend that you are a young, eager newspaper reporter. You have been given the job of finding this person, interviewing him, and doing your very first front-page story.
3. Reporters in the 1870s did not have the luxury of a photographer, therefore, you must make sketches to go along with your story.
4. When you have gathered the necessary information and pictures, write the first draft of your newspaper story. Be sure to include an exciting headline. Use colorful language and be factual, yet dramatic, in your approach.
5. Edit, revise, and print out the final copy of the news story.

Men of the West

- Buffalo Bill Cody
- Davy Crockett
- Merriwether Lewis
- James Bridger
- John Fremont
- William Becknell

- George Vancouver
- Marcus Whitman
- Kit Carson
- John Wesley Powell
- Stephen Austin
- Charles Goodnight

- William Clark
- Zebulon Pike
- Samuel Houston
- Wild Bill Hickok
- Daniel Boone
- Wyatt Earp

Name: _____ Date: _____

The Dispossessed People

Assignment Guidelines

This week you will be looking at what happened to Native Americans during the time when the West was being settled. You will choose one tribe, research how they were affected by white settlers, and write a letter to governmental leaders to inform them of your plight and ask for specific rights or considerations. This is what you will do:

1. Research the settlement of the West and generally how this affected native people living in these areas. Choose one specific tribe and find out what happened to them when settlers moved into their homelands.
2. Pretend that you are leader of this tribe and it is your responsibility to try to find an amiable agreement with the white settlers that will protect your people's rights to live on and hunt or farm on lands you have occupied for hundreds of years.
3. Write a letter to the leaders of the white people explaining the following things:
   a. Who you are and where you live
   b. How your tribe has used the land for hunting, farming, fishing, or trading
   c. What problems the western expansion is causing your tribe
   d. How you feel about the present conditions
   e. What you feel would be a fair compromise
   f. What you want the government to do about it
4. You may include a map showing the territory of where you live.
5. Revise and edit your letter and write it in a proper letter format.

Native Americans and Western Expansion

In 1830, the Indian Removal Act authorized the removal of eastern tribes to locations west of the Mississippi. Then in 1862, Congress passed the Homestead Act, promising farmers free land. This started a wave of settlers rushing into the West. These two acts confirmed the right of settlers to move Native Americans wherever they found them, so as people moved west, Native Americans were pushed out of their lands. Some of the tribes resisted invasion, attacking settlers and fighting the cavalry, and some just gave up their land for territory farther west (from which they were often later evicted). By 1890, no Native American titles to land were left, and the Native American population had been largely restricted to reservations on land of poor quality.

Name: _____ Date: _____

Come to America, Land of Opportunity

Assignment Guidelines

This week, you will be working with a partner to find out about life in the United States at the turn of the twentieth century and make a poster to attract people to this land of opportunity.

1. Research the following things about the U.S. in the year 1900. While the information may be hard to locate, find as much as you can.
   a. The population of the U.S.
   b. The number and distribution of immigrants
   c. Populations of New York, Philadelphia, and Chicago
   d. The main occupations
   e. The general distribution of farms and industries
   f. The major universities
   g. The modes of transportation, nationwide and in the large cities
   h. The status of public schools and the mandatory age for education
2. Once you have the information, display it on the poster in an attractive manner. Illustrations should accompany each section. The poster is meant to attract immigrants to the United States from other parts of the world.
3. Finally, present the poster to the class, showing the aspects of life you chose to portray on your poster.

Name: _____ Date: _____

Silent Movie Making

Assignment Guidelines

This week you will complete the following assignments:

1. You will work with a group to research a topic and write a script for a silent movie.
2. The script should portray a period in history in which something dramatic happened.
3. Include some dialogue in your script that will be written on large pieces of paper. The day of filming, these strips will be held up in front of the camera as the words are mouthed silently by the actors.
4. All members of your group must have at least one acting part. It is very important that you act with gestures and be very dramatic in your presentation, for there is no spoken dialogue.
5. All silent movies had a musical background that continued for the duration of the film. Select an appropriate musical accompaniment for your presentation.
6. Present your movie for the class.

About Silent Films

Edison's invention of the kinetoscope in 1894 and the vitascope in 1896 led to the first projected motion picture, *The Great Train Robbery,* in 1903. This led to the establishment of nickelodeons and finally to movie palaces. By 1913, the film industry was well established and growing, though it wasn't until 1927 that a film with sound was released. That film was *The Jazz Singer.*

Suggestions for Scripts

- Marco Polo's meeting with Kublai Khan
- Completion of the great pyramid of Giza
- The Boston Tea Party
- Bell's invention of the telephone
- The fall of the Berlin Wall
- The landing on the moon
- Completion of the transcontinental railroad
- An explorer's discovery of new land or a new passage
- Napoleon's final defeat at Waterloo
- A scene depicting the first women's rights convention
- Carter's discovery of King Tut's tomb
- A civil rights march
- Women getting to vote for president for the first time
- Lee's surrender to Grant at Appomattox Courthouse
- Lewis and Clark's encounter with a group of Native Americans on their journey in the West

Name: _____ Date: _____

Revolutionary Transportation

Assignment Guidelines

This week you will be working with a partner on the following assignments:

1. Research and take notes on the following subjects:
    a. One of the first automobiles
    b. One of the first airplanes
    c. A modern automobile
    d. A modern airplane (either a passenger or private plane)
2. Find out the following information about the automobiles and airplanes you have selected:

Automobile	**Airplane**
• Exterior structure	• Size
• Interior design	• Structural materials
• Type of engine	• Interior design
• Accessories	• Engine design

3. After you have gathered all the information, make drawings of the two automobiles you researched and the two airplanes you researched—a total of four drawings.
4. Finally, use your notes and drawings to write a paper comparing the four vehicles you have studied. Write about the automobiles first, comparing the old model to the new one. Then compare the two models of airplanes. Include both the similarities and differences. Note which items or parts of the machines changed the least over the years and which changed the most. Tell how you think the goals of automobile and airplane designers have changed over the years.

Early Airplanes

   In 1820, Cayley invented the first flying glider, and in 1842 Henson developed the steam-powered airplane. The first successful controlled airplane flight was made by the Wright brothers in 1903. Within just a few years, there were many competing manufacturers. Aircraft technology was further stimulated by World War I and has continued to make advancements since then.

Early Automobiles

   The first gas-powered automobile was developed in the mid-1880s by Benz and Daimler. In 1893, the Duryea brothers made the first American automobile. Henry Ford began manufacturing automobiles in 1903, pioneering the first cheap, mass-produced Model T in 1908.

Name: _____ Date: _____

African-American Heroes

Assignment Guidelines

This week you will be finding out about a great African American who lived some time in our country's history.

1. Find as much information as you can about the person who has been assigned to you.
2. Compile a set of materials that are representative of this person. Include personal statements, newspaper articles, letters, awards, illustrations, or any other things a person might collect to document his or her accomplishments.
3. Place all the materials in a portfolio that you will present to the class.
4. For your presentation, you will pretend that you are interviewing for a job. You will present your very best work, writings, photos, and symbols or objects pertaining to your life, and you will explain each item.
5. Work with a partner who will be your interviewer. Likewise, you will interview your partner, so he or she can share the contents of his or her portfolio.

Sample Contents

If you were assigned Martin Luther King, Jr., you might prepare some of the following writings:
- A brief autobiography, telling about his life
- A resumé, listing his education, the jobs he has had, and his most important accomplishments
- A written statement of his philosophy
- An editorial he might have written for a newspaper
- Some pictures or symbols of his life

Prominent African Americans

- Langston Hughes
- Shirley Chisolm
- Malcolm X
- Ralph David Abernathy
- Frederick Douglass
- James Baldwin
- Adam Clayton Powell
- Condoleezza Rice

- Lewis Hayden
- Edward W. Brooke
- Jesse Owens
- Jackie Robinson
- Harriet Tubman
- Thurgood Marshall
- Ralph J. Bunche
- Barack Obama

- Daniel Hale Williams
- Louis Armstrong
- Charles White
- Charles Drew
- W. E. B. DuBois
- Mary McLeod Bethune
- Colin Powell
- Martin Luther King, Jr.

Name: _____   Date: _____

Famous Women

Assignment Guidelines

This week you will be researching an American woman who has made a worthwhile contribution and gained fame and also interviewing a woman in your life whom you admire. You will then compare these two women.

1. Choose and research an American woman.
2. Choose another woman whom you know and admire and whom you could interview some time this week. If you cannot find a person to interview, you can research two famous women and compare these two women.
3. Write questions that you will use to interview the woman in your own life. Adapt your interview questions to reflect some of the events that occurred in the woman's life whom you researched. For instance, if your famous person was poor as a child, one of the questions you could ask in your interview is, "In your childhood, do you remember being rich, poor, or average?" Ask detailed questions that will get meaningful responses.
4. Finally, draw a comparison between the two women by writing a paper in which you list likenesses and differences between these two women. You should not so much compare accomplishments as goals, interests, upbringing, or education. Explain the admirable qualities of both women.

Sample Interview Questions

1. If you could become any one woman who has lived in America, past or present, for one day, who would you choose? Tell me some reasons why you chose her.
2. Describe your childhood using just five words.
3. Now take each word you gave me in the last question and tell me the reasons you chose each word.
4. If you could go into any profession at this time in your life, no matter what the cost, what would you choose and why?
5. Tell me one change you would make in your life if you could.
6. Tell me what your dream for the future is.

Notable Women

- Eleanor Roosevelt
- Lucy Stone
- Amelia Earhart
- Margaret Mead
- Sally Ride
- Rachel Carson
- Rosa Parks
- Clara Barton
- Sandra Day O'Conner
- Catherine Beecher
- Mary McLeod Bethune
- Elizabeth Cady Stanton
- Madeleine Albright
- Elizabeth Blackwell

Name: _____ Date: _____

Comparing Presidents

Assignment Guidelines

This week you will be working with a partner to find information about two presidents of the United States. Then you will write a speech for each president and compare the leaders on several points. Here is a list of your assignments for the week:

1. Choose the presidents that you want to research.
2. Do research on each of these men. You may research together or each of you may do research separately on a different person. You will want to find out the following about each, although any interesting information may be added.
   a. Birthplace
   b. Childhood
   c. Education
   d. Early political career
   e. Marriage and family
   f. Campaign for presidency
   g. The difficulties faced during his term
   h. Domestic and foreign policies

3. After you complete the research, write a speech as if you are the president's biographer, telling about the president's life and accomplishments. Write one speech for each president.
4. Each person will present one of the presidents. At the end of the two speeches, come together in front of the class and present a comparison of the presidents, pointing out similarities and differences.

Sample Speech

     Good evening, and thank you for your kind applause. It is so good to be here this evening to tell you about the life and presidency of John F. Kennedy. Mr. Kennedy served as president from 1960 until 1963 when he was assassinated by Lee Harvey Oswald in Dallas, Texas.

     He was born in Massachusetts. His parents were Joseph and Rose Kennedy. They had a very large and very close family.

Name: _____   Date: _____

Propaganda

Assignment Guidelines

This week you will be learning about various types of propaganda techniques. You will then make a poster depicting several of these techniques. Here is your list of assignments.

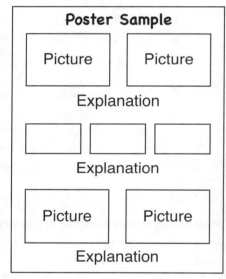

1. Research different propaganda techniques.
2. Go through magazines and newspapers to find as many examples of each technique as you can. Cut these out, group them according to the type of propaganda they demonstrate, and glue them to poster board.
3. Underneath each category, write an explanation of the type of propaganda used.
4. Finally, share this poster with the class, giving reasons why you believe each picture shows a particular type of propaganda.

Definition of Propaganda

Propaganda is selective information (true or false) used to persuade people to adopt a particular belief, attitude or course of action. It has been used by political parties, as a tool of war, and by advertising and public relations campaigns.

Types of Propaganda

1. **Glittering Generalities** – This propaganda technique provides glowing claims but nothing to back up the claims. For instance, "This is the best car on the road."
2. **Card Stacking** – This type uses only part of the facts to make a favorable point. For example, saying "Nine out of ten dentists surveyed favored WhiteTeeth toothpaste" when the survey did not question a large sampling of dentists.
3. **Just Plain Folks** – In this type, the person tells people he/she is just like them. For example, "I was raised right here in Sweetrock, so you know I'll look out for your best interests."
4. **Name Calling** – This type attaches negative labels on other products or opponents. For example, "As you all know, Charlie Smith has a rather questionable past."
5. **Bandwagon** – This plays on the fear people have of being left out. For example, "Anyone who skis, skis at Glitterdome!"
6. **Transfer** – This type of propaganda tries to identify with a famous person. For example, "Our company was built on the ideas of Abraham Lincoln."

Poster Sample

Picture	Picture

Explanation

Explanation

Picture	Picture

Explanation

Fact & Opinion

Assignment Guidelines

For this week's lesson, you will do the following assignments:

1. Begin by studying the national and local events reported in a newspaper, news magazine, or an online news site. Then write at least 20 questions based on the news events. The questions should ask two things: What are the facts and what is your opinion about the situation? As you write, be sure that an opinionated answer can be given for the question. You should know the answers to the factual questions. For example, two questions regarding an upcoming presidential election might be:
    a. **Fact** – Who will be running for president in the next election?
    b. **Opinion** – In your opinion, who is the best candidate and why do you think this?
2. After you have written your questions, interview a partner, having the partner answer all the questions. Record your partner's answers carefully.
3. Finally, study the answers your partner gave you and write an essay about this experience, following the additional guidelines in the box below.

Fact or Opinion

Fact – Something known to exist or to have happened; a truth known by actual experience or observation

Opinion – A belief, judgment, or personal attitude

Essay Guidelines

When you write your essay about your interviewing experience, answer the following questions:

1. Was your partner well-informed?
2. Which questions did your partner find especially difficult to answer?
3. Did you find anything out about the way you worded your questions that could help you write better questions next time?
4. Which questions were your best ones? Worst ones?
5. Which questions, the fact or opinion questions, demanded more interesting answers? Why do you think this?

Name: _____   Date: _____

Points of View

Assignment Guidelines

Throughout history, people have had different points of view that showed their biased opinions about a wide variety of issues. These differences have sometimes led to serious disagreements and resulted in large-scale wars. Sometimes, though, differences have only provided material for debate and gradual social change. Being able to see the other person's point of view helps you seek solutions that are mutually acceptable. For this week's lesson, you will be choosing a situation that has two different points of view and will write a dialogue that shows those two viewpoints. Here is what you will do:

1. Choose a historic event or period in which there was a conflict. Research this topic thoroughly so that you understand what the conflict was and what the two different points of view were.
2. Divide a piece of paper in half vertically and label each half with the name of the two opposing people or groups. In each column, write statements that express that group's point of view.
3. Choose two people or create two fictional people who would represent each viewpoint.
4. Write an introductory paragraph that describes the situation, the time period, and the location. Then write a dialogue between the two people in which each one expresses his or her point of view and tries to make the other person understand this perspective. Close with a paragraph in which you suggest how these two people could resolve the conflict or find common ground.
5. Choose a classmate to help you read the dialogue in an oral presentation.

Possible Research Topics

- The Reformation
- The American Revolution
- The Mexican-American War
- The Civil Rights Movement
- The colonization of the New World
- Sending humans into space
- The use of child labor during the Industrial Revolution
- The internment of Japanese Americans during World War II

- Women's suffrage
- Emancipation
- The French Revolution
- The Haymarket Riots
- Formation of Labor Unions
- U.S. involvement in the Vietnam War

- Prohibition
- The Crusades
- Feudalism
- Apartheid

Name: _____ Date: _____

Migration

Assignment Guidelines

This week you will be looking at the concept of migration. You will be selecting a specific time in history when people migrated from one area to the other and will base your project on this migration. This is what you will do this week:

1. Choose a time during history when you can find a group of people who migrated from one place to another. Study this time and these people to find out where they came from, why they wanted to leave, where they went, and what they encountered when they arrived in their new location.

2. Draw a map that shows two locations, where the people came from and where they migrated to, and the route that they followed. Write the date or dates when this migration took place on the map.

3. Write an explanation of the migration that includes the following facts:
   a. Who the people were
   b. Where they came from
   c. Why they wanted to leave this place
   d. Where they went
   e. What they encountered in their new location

4. Mount the map and the explanation on a large piece of paper and label the project with an appropriate title.

5. Share your project with the class, explaining what was gained and what was lost with this migration.

A Historical Perspective

Throughout recorded history, people have migrated from one place to another. Their reasons for migrating have been varied: looking for better hunting or farming, seeking religious freedom, escaping war, taking advantage of free land, or looking for wealth. Some of these migrations have included:

- People crossing the land bridge from Asia to North America
- Europeans migrating to America seeking religious freedom or escaping tough economic conditions in their home countries
- People in the eastern U.S. migrating to the West and Southwest in the 1800s
- People moving from farms to cities during the Industrial Revolution
- Jewish people fleeing Germany during World War II
- People in Southeast Asia leaving their homelands following the Vietnam War

Name: _____ Date: _____

Earth Geography

Day 1: Earth Geography

For your first assignment this week, you will imagine that as you prepare for bed, there is a tap on your window, and you see a being from another planet right outside your room. Your visitor wants to know everything about the planet Earth. It is your job to write a description, telling him about Earth's geography. Include:

- Names and placement of continents
- Various land formations
- Names of the oceans
- Where you live

Day 2: Your Home Town

Now your alien friend wants to take you on a trip around your town. He is able to fly close to the ground so you can tell him everything you see. You will need to plan where you will go and what you will tell him about each place. Write the things you will say to the alien as you fly together. Tell him about the special sights and landforms. Find a good spot for lunch where you will be able to point out lots of interesting things.

Day 3: Three Favorite Places

Use maps to locate three places you would like to visit. Before you begin this writing, locate several types of maps of your selected area, like:

- Climate maps
- Resource or product maps
- Maps showing forests
- Physical maps
- Population maps
- Political maps
- Mineral deposit maps

Then describe the places you would like to visit. When you write about the three places you would like to visit, include several facts about the places by using information from all the maps you found.

Day 4: A Favorite State

Draw a map of your favorite state on a large piece of paper. Indicate the various landforms, the type of weather it has, rivers, cities, towns and parks in the state. You should also represent the products or crops produced in the state, the population, and the forests, minerals, and fossil fuels. Create a set of symbols to represent the things on your map.

Day 5: Revision

When you have completed all the work for this project, take your best piece of writing and prepare it for publication. Revise the piece to make it as good as possible. Then edit it for spelling, capitalization, and punctuation. Type it or write it in your very best handwriting.

Name: _____ Date: _____

Regions of Our Country

Assignment Guidelines

The regions of the United States that you will be studying are the **Northeast**, **Southeast**, **Southwest**, **Midwest**, and the **West**. Complete the following tasks and place your findings on or near the map in the classroom.

Group 1 will find the natural resources of each region, make symbols of each resource, and glue or staple them to the large map in the appropriate places.

Group 2 will find the largest cities of each region, label each city on the map, and make a symbol to represent the city.

Group 3 will study the agricultural products of each region, make symbols for the main products, and attach them to the map in the appropriate places.

Group 4 will study the climate maps of each region, make a chart showing the general climate of each region (with illustrations), then tape or staple it in a place outside of the actual map with an arrow pointing to the region.

Group 5 will study the land formations of each region, make small pictures of these formations, and put these on the map where they are actually located or outside of the map with an arrow pointing to where they are located.

Group 6 will study landmarks, national parks, major tourist attractions, and historic sites found in each region, make little pictures of these things, and attach these to the map.

A Comparison of the Regions

When you complete the assignment with your group, make a diagram of five ovals. List the general characteristics of each region in an oval.

Climate Comparison

Climate of the West

Climate of the Midwest

Climate of the Northeast

Climate of the Southwest

Climate of the Southeast

Name: _____ Date: _____

Time Traveler

Assignment Guidelines

This week you will be writing a story about traveling through time from one period in history into another period in history. It is important that you know what life was like in both time periods. It is easiest if you choose one time period that you have studied previously and another time period that you are studying now. Your writing will be in three different parts, each part set in a different time and place. The three parts of your paper will be:

1. The first will explain the time machine, how you built the time machine, found the time machine, or discovered the time machine. Describe the machine, tell how it works, what color it is, what lights it emits, and what sounds it makes.
2. The second part of your writing will be set in the place and time from which you begin your journey. For instance, you may want to begin in the colonial period and travel to the Civil War period, or begin in ancient Egypt and go to the Middle Ages. In this case, you would describe your surroundings in the colonial period or in ancient Egypt in detail.
3. The third setting will be where you travel to in the time machine. Describe this time and place and tell about the exciting events that occur there.

Example

   My great adventure began one morning as I took my Saturday trash-hunt stroll. The cobblestone streets were deserted because of the early hour, but I was eager to find new treasures. I came around the corner of the old Gleeson place that had been abandoned for years and was surprised to find an old dilapidated contraption sitting in the gutter. It had wheels and tires and dials and wires sticking out in all directions. It was all rusted and squeaked everywhere. It was surprisingly lightweight, so I proceeded to drag it home.

   After the machine was all repaired and shone with a brand new paint job, I decided to get into the seat and try it out. My mother said first I had to go up the street to Thomas Jefferson and give him some pepper jelly that she made with the peppers he gave her from his garden. He is famous for his garden and also for writing the Declaration of Independence, which Mother said would one day be a great piece of history.

Name: _____ Date: _____

A Snowy Adventure

Assignment Guidelines

This week you will use your imagination to write a story that takes place sometime in history on a cold, snowy day or night. You can use the standard story format or you can make your story like a diary or journal.

1. Your story is to take place on a cold, snowy day or night.
2. The story must take place sometime in the past (your favorite period in history or the period of history that you are studying at this time) and include action and adventure.
3. You must include details that speak to the senses (taste, touch, smell, sight, and hearing).
4. Write a rough draft. Then revise and edit it completely so that it is free of errors.
5. Then write a final draft.
6. Share your story with your group.

Two Sample Beginnings

It was late, Mother told us it would be very cold that night and we should draw our bed closer to the fire. My little brother and I cuddled beneath the thick cover that was stuffed full of goose feathers. In a short time, we were as warm as toast. George quickly fell asleep, but I lay awake watching the flames dance on the hearth. Soon, I too, was asleep. I was suddenly awakened for no reason and noticed a warm glow coming from the windows. It was as if the moon had become many times brighter. I made my way toward the window. Then I saw what caused the brightness. It was snowing. The world lay white, all white, before my eyes! I slipped over to the bed and whispered ever so softly, "Guess what! It's snowing!" George jumped out of the bed and flew to the window. We both dressed quickly and silently and made our way outside to be the first to mark the snow. It was bitterly cold, and as we leaped and slipped down the slopes, the snow wet our faces and turned our cheeks and noses rosy.

Father asked me to take a letter to Mr. Revere's house that night, but he didn't know it had snowed. I dressed warmly and started off through the streets of Boston to the harbor area. The snow licked my nose and mouth. As I passed Mr. Adam's house, I stopped to take a mound of snow from the top of his fence. I proceeded to eat it and the icy cold sliced through me. When I arrived at the Reveres', the windows were warmly lit with the firelight inside. I knocked at the door and was admitted. Mrs. Revere took me to the soft chair nearest the fire and brought me crisp sugar cookies and steamy hot tea. When they were assured that I had thoroughly thawed, they sent me home with a little package of cookies for the family.

Name: _____ Date: _____

A Yard Sale Treasure

Assignment Guidelines

This week you will be using what you know about the state of affairs in our own country and in the world to make a list of wishes to make the world a better place. Here are the assignments for the week:

1. First, list all the things that you want to make better in our own country or around the world. Just list them randomly, with no particular order.
2. Choose the top five wishes.
3. Write your wishes and then plan out a very detailed procedure for attaining these wishes. For example: My wish for the world is that all students in the U.S. would make education their main goal in life. The way I would accomplish my goal is I would first get funding for my project. Then I would purchase time on all the major broadcasting systems and the social media outlets on the Internet. I would do research about the difference in the life of someone who has been educated in comparison to someone who has not. I would put all my findings in the ads. I would also use the ads to tell the students how other children across the world feel about education. I would get big rock stars to tell why education is so important.
4. Finally, write a story using the fictional premise in the box below.

Story Premise

One Saturday morning, you wake up and decide to do your favorite thing, look for treasures at local yard sales. You hop on your bike and set off. You come to an alley with dark Victorian houses on each side. You see a sign painted in red, "Attic Sale, Treasures Old and New." You park the bike and open the tall unpainted gate leading to the yard. There, sitting in an antique rocker is an old wrinkled lady. Then you see it! A tarnished trinket box. You bargain and get it for a good price.

When you arrive home, you take the box to the basement and rummage through the cleaners and chemicals until you find the brass polish. You rub the box, and suddenly the box pops open and POOF! Out jumps a miniature man with a long, snowy white beard. He tells you that he is your genie and that you will be granted five wishes. He says he has to have specific directions about each of your five wishes or he will not grant them. So you think and think until you come up with your list of five wishes and plans for accomplishing the wishes.

Name: _____ Date: _____

Designing the Future

Assignment Guidelines

This week, you will be planning a city of the future. You will work in groups to accomplish the following tasks:

1. Pretend that it is the year 2030. You are a very intelligent and successful person who now works for the government. You have just been called into the office of the new Director of Cities. She explains that the government has set aside funds for a brand new city to be built. This city will be a model for other cities in terms of using current technology and prudent urban design to solve problems that currently exist in other cities. Your job is to work with a team of brilliant young men and women to come up with a design for this city.
2. Discuss the probable needs of the people in the year 2030 and come up with a design for a future city. You can place your city anywhere in the country.
3. Make a map and pictures of the city, color them, and display them in an attractive way.
4. Write an accompanying explanation of each part of the city and how it will function.

Important Considerations

The following are some things to keep in mind as you design the city of the future:

1. Remember that the population of cities will grow by the year 2030. How will you house these people?
2. You must include a transportation system that is energy efficient. If you design an energy system that runs on garbage or nuclear energy, you must dispose of the waste materials.
3. You must include an area for children. Assume that it will be so expensive to live that it will be necessary for both parents to work full time.
4. Schooling must be a part of your design; however, you may choose to have students educated in ways that are different from our present school-based format.
5. Crime probably will not decrease in the future. What measures will you take to keep crime under control?
6. You must also consider recreation. How will you provide entertainment for your inhabitants?

Acknowledgments

With thanks to my husband Ron, not only for his outstanding illustrations that bring each page to life, but also for his love and support.

To my mother, my first great teacher.

To my brother Steve for his editing and loving encouragement.

To Judy Barry for her never-ending faith in me.

To the Sisters of Saint Joseph, wonderful educators.

To Ms. Culmer for her belief and example.

~Joyce Stulgis Blalock, author